The Door Is Open

Tana Reiff

A Pacemaker **LifeTimes™ 2** Book

The Door Is Open

Tana Reiff
AR B.L.: 2.7
Points: 0.5   UG

GLOBE FEARON

Pearson Learning Group

LifeTimes™ 2 Titles

Take Away Three
Climbing the Wall
The Door Is Open
Just for Today
Chicken by Che
Play Money
The Missing Piece

Cover illustration: Michaela Cooney

ISBN 0-8224-4604-9
Printed in the United States of America

5 6 7 8 9 10 11   06 05 04 03 02

Globe
Fearon
Pearson Learning Group

1-800-321-3106
www.pearsonlearning.com

Contents

CHAPTER 1

Lina looked up
at the door.
The sign said,
"Adult School.
Everyone Welcome."

She walked inside.
She had wanted
to return
to school
for many years.
Now she was here.
Now she was afraid.
She had not
gone to school
for 22 years.

She opened the door.
She walked inside
the school.

"What is
your name?"
asked the woman
at the front desk.

"Lina Conti,"
said the new student.

The woman
wrote it down.

"Did you
finish high school?"
asked the woman.

"No,"
answered Lina.
"I stopped
going to school
when I was 16.
I never went
to school
in all my years
in America."

"Where do you
come from?"
asked the woman.

"Italy,"
answered Lina.
"I have been
in America
for 22 years.
When I was 16
I was brought here
to be married."

"Your English
is very good,"
said the woman.

"Not good enough,"
said Lina.
"I want to speak
better English.
I also want
to get my
high school diploma."

"Why now?"
asked the woman.

"My children are
almost grown up,"
said Lina.
"They are
almost finished with school.
I am a member
of many groups.
Church groups.
City groups.
I do a lot of work
for other people.
Now it's my turn.
I want
to learn.
I want to be
good enough
to get a good job."

"Ready when
you are,"
said the woman.

"I'm ready,"
said Lina.
"Just one more thing.
My husband
doesn't know
I'm here.
Please don't
tell him."

Thinking It Over

1. People have many reasons
   for not finishing school.
   How many can you think of?

2. When is a good time
   to return to school?

3. Why do you think
   Lina doesn't want her husband
   to know she is going to school?

CHAPTER 2

Lina still remembered
Italy every day.
She remembered the hills
where she grew up.
The air
was clean.
There were
only blue skies
and mountains
all around.
Life was simple.

Then Lina's uncle
went to America.
He wrote back
that he had found
a husband
for Lina
in America.
His name
was Alonzo Conti.

But the young girl
didn't want
to leave her home.
She was only 16.
Alonzo was 28.

"Your life
will be full of joy,"
her mother told her.
"You will have
children and money.
You will have
a good life
in America.
You must go."

So Lina went
to America.
She went on a boat
all by herself.

Alonzo had
his own business.
He sold cars.

Even 22 years ago
he was making
good money.

Al and Lina
got married.
In the next few years
they had four beautiful children.
They lived
in a big, pretty house.
Lina wore
nice clothes.
Lina did not have to work
outside the home.
She and Al
were very happy together.
They had
a happy family.

But money
did not give Lina
everything she wanted.
Until now
her whole life

was Al's life.
Now she needed
to do something
for herself.
She needed
to reach a goal
of her own.
"The door was open
for Al,"
she said to herself.
"Now maybe it will open
for me, too."

Thinking It Over

1. Is the "door"
    open to everyone?
    Why or why not?

2. Should Lina be happy enough
    with what she already has?

3. What makes you happy?

CHAPTER 3

Adult school
was the first open door.
Lina loved it.
She was surprised
at how fast
she could learn.

"You speak English
pretty well,"
Liz, the teacher,
told her.
"That's why
it's easy for you
to learn
to read English.
But how do you know
so much math?"

"I keep
the books

for my husband's business,"
said Lina.

   "I see,"
said Liz.
"You already knew
a lot of the stuff
we're doing in class.
You're just opening
the door
of your mind!"

   Most of all,
Lina enjoyed
learning about English.
It was interesting
to know
why certain verbs
go in certain places.
She saw
that she
had been using
some verbs
in the wrong places.

Lina really enjoyed
learning to spell.
She knew
most of the words.
But she had never
seen them
in print.

Speaking and reading
were beginning
to come together for Lina.
She became
the best student
in the class.
She felt great.
She didn't feel afraid.

Thinking It Over

1. Lina learned math
    by doing her husband's books.
    What have you learned to do
    without going to school?

2. What is a verb?

3. What makes a good student?

CHAPTER 4

"Where do you go
every day?"
Al wanted to know.

Lina could never
lie to her husband.
"I go to school,"
she said.

"To school?"
said Al.
"What for?
You have everything
you need.
The kids are
older now.
Take it easy.
Take up a sport."

"I want
to finish school,"

said Lina.
"I want a diploma.
What's wrong
with that?"

"I never
finished school,"
Al said.
"I don't have
a diploma.
But I made it anyway.
Besides,
a woman's place
is still at home."

"Oh, come on,"
said Lina.
"Times have changed.
You don't still
believe that,
do you?"

"Yes, I do,"
said Al.
"But I also

need you
to help me run
my car business."

   "You got to choose
your own life,"
said Lina.
"You chose
to come to America.
You chose
to sell cars.
I never had
a choice.
The choice
was made for me.
I was brought here
and that was that."

   "Your life
isn't so bad,"
said Al.

   "My life
is very nice,"
said Lina.

"But I want
to finish school.
This is something
I really want to do.
What's wrong
with that?"

Al said nothing.
He didn't look happy.

Thinking It Over

1. Why is Al
    acting the way he is?

2. Is there any reason
    that someone should *not*
    finish school?

3. How have "times changed"
    since you've been alive?

CHAPTER 5

Lina kept on
going to school.
To get her diploma,
she studied
math, reading, and English.
Her favorite class
was still English.

In fact,
Lina was so good
at English
that she helped
other students.
There were students
from many countries.
Lina got along
with everyone.
And everyone
liked Lina.

Every year
the school
had a big party.
It was time
for this year's party.
Everyone brought
something to eat.
There were foods
from all over
the world.

Lina made
an Italian dish.
Everyone said
it tasted very good.

Then the students
started to dance.
Lina joined in.
She hadn't danced
since she
got married.
Some of the music
was strange

to her.
But she enjoyed herself.

    Then Lina said,
"Let me teach you
a dance.
This is
a dance
that I did
as a girl
in Italy."

    Lina showed everyone
her dance.
They followed
her feet.
Then everyone
joined in
with her.
It was
almost like
being back
in Italy.

Thinking It Over

1. What makes you think
   of the place you grew up?

2. What can you learn
   from people from other places?

3. Why does a person like Lina
   get along well
   with everyone?

CHAPTER 6

The diploma test
was coming up soon.
Lina became
afraid again.
She wanted
to pass the test.

"You'll make it,"
said Liz, the teacher.

"I hope so,"
said Lina.
"But even if I pass,
Al will be angry
with me.
He still doesn't think
going to school
is a good idea."

The night
before the test,

Lina wanted
to study at home.
"I'll have to hide
these books
in my bag,"
she told Liz.

Liz shook
her head.
"Maybe someday
Al will understand,"
she said.

But that night
Al found
Lina's schoolbooks.
He was angry.
"Why are you
doing this to me?"
he asked her.

"I'm not
doing anything
against you,"
said Lina.

"I don't understand
what you need
a diploma for,"
Al said.

"I want to feel
I have reached
my goal,"
Lina answered.

"Tomorrow
I need you
at the car lot,"
Al said.

"I'll come
to the car lot,"
said Lina.
"But not until
I finish the test."

Al shook his head
and walked
out of the room.

Thinking It Over

1. How is Lina
    standing up for herself?

2. Why does all of this
    make Al angry?

3. Would you go to school
    if someone you loved
    didn't want you to?

CHAPTER 7

It was Saturday.
This was the day
of the diploma test.

Lina woke up
very early.
The sun was
just coming up.
She got dressed.
She wrote a note
for Al.
"Meet you
at the car lot,"
it said.
She left the note
on the kitchen table.

Then she
left the house
without making a sound.

She walked
all the way
to the school.
She had to take
that test.
In her heart
she knew
she could pass it.
But the rest
of her body
was shaking.

She got to the school
very early.
She was
the first one there.
She looked
at her books
one last time.

One by one
the other students
got to the school.
Lina helped them
with last-minute studying.

She made them
feel better
about the test.

A bell rang.
Everyone went inside
and took a seat.
It was time
to begin the test.

Lina didn't think
about Al.
She put her mind
on the test.
She tried to remember
what Liz had said.
"Don't take
a break.
Don't take
too much time
on one question.
Don't leave
any blank spaces.
Guess the answer
if you don't know it.

Keep your eye
on the clock.
And be sure to follow
all the rules."

Time went fast.
And then
the test was over.

Lina took a bus
to the car lot.
Once again,
Al said nothing.
Lina could tell
he was not happy.

Thinking It Over

1. Do you think that Lina
    should have gone
    to take the test?

2. How can you tell
    Lina was ready
    to take the diploma test?

3. When does time
    seem to go fast for you?

CHAPTER 8

Who would pass
the test?
The list came out
the next Friday.

Al had not talked
about the test
all week.
Lina had not said
anything about it.
She had not told
the children about it, either.
She didn't want
to put them
on the spot
with their father.

Lina called
the school.
"Did I pass?"
she asked Liz.

"Didn't you hear?
You passed!"
said Liz.
"Your husband called
and asked me.
So I told him."
Lina could hear Liz
clapping her hands.

"And guess what, Lina?"
Liz added.
"You had
a very high score.
Did you ever think
about going to college?"

"I would love
to go to college,"
said Lina.
"But Al would
never let me
do that.
He would have to pay
for it.
And he would never

want to pay
for me
to go to college."

"Work on him,"
said Liz.
"And let's talk
more about it later."

Lina looked
out the window.
There was Al.
He was driving
a new car
from his lot.

"I must hang up,"
Lina told Liz.
"Al is home
in the middle
of the day.
Maybe something
is wrong."

But nothing was wrong.
Al had a surprise

for Lina.
"Come and see
your new car!"
he called.
"It's your graduation present.
I thought about it
all week.
I was being selfish.
It's good that
you went
back to school.
Better late
than never.
I hope
you like
your new car!"

Al was happy
for Lina after all.
That made Lina
very happy, too.
She drove the car
around the block.

Thinking It Over

1. Why do you think
    Al gave Lina
    such a nice present?

2. What could have changed
    Al's mind?

3. What does it mean
    to be put "on the spot"?

CHAPTER 9

After Lina
finished school,
she spent
more time
at the car lot.

One day
she brought up
the idea
of going to college.
Al looked surprised
and a little hurt.

"I'm not trying
to get ahead
of you,"
explained Lina.
"This is just something
I need to do.
I opened the door

of learning.
Now I don't want
to close it."

"What about
the kids?"
asked Al.
"What about
the house?"

"I can handle
everything,"
said Lina.
"The kids
can take care
of themselves now.
They help
around the house.
Even so,
the house
doesn't have to be
so clean
all the time."

"And what about
my business?"

asked Al.
"I need you
to do these books."

"Don't worry,"
said Lina.
"I'll do the books.
I'll just have to
plan my time.
I can go
to college
part-time at first."

Al laughed.
"There is
no stopping you,
is there?
If you really want to go,
I can't stop you."

"Thank you,"
said Lina.
"I hope someday
you will understand
why I want
to go to college."

Thinking It Over

1.   How do you think
     Lina will handle
     everything she wants to do?

2.   Why is Al
     against the idea of college?

3.   When you really want
     to do something,
     can anyone stop you?
     Is that good or bad?

CHAPTER 10

There was a college
near Lina's home.
Lina met
with a man there.
His job
was to talk
to new students.
He asked Lina
about her interests.

"I loved
studying English,"
she told him.
"I loved learning
English grammar.
And I loved helping
the other students."

"That's interesting,"
said the man.

"What kind of job
would you like?"

"To be a teacher,"
said Lina.
"But I still don't speak
like an American."

"That might not
be a problem,"
said the man.
"Maybe you could teach
English as a second language.
You could study
to become a teacher.
Then you could teach English
to other people.
What do you think
about that idea?"

"I love the idea,"
said Lina.
"Do you really think
I could do that?"

"You have
very good test scores,"
said the man.
"Yes, I think
you could become
a teacher.
You could study
right here
at this college.
You would be
very close to home."

Once again,
everything
was beginning
to come together.

Thinking It Over

1.   Why would Lina
     make a good teacher?

2.   What could Lina
     do about going to school
     if there weren't a college
     near her home?

3.   Why would someone
     want to begin college
     as a part-time student?

CHAPTER 11

When fall came,
Lina started college.
She began
with only two courses.
She didn't want
to get in
over her head.

She also took
another test.
This test
gave her points
for things
she already knew.
These points
let her pass
three courses
without ever going
to class.

The college classes
were not easy.
But for some reason
Lina was not afraid.
She knew
that if she worked hard
she could make it.

Sometimes she felt
much older
than the other students.
Most of them
were 18 years old.
Lina was old enough
to be their mother.
But she didn't act
like their mother.
She acted
like herself.
That is why
the other students
liked her.

And she got along
very well

with the teachers.
Most of them
were close
to her age.

Al was not
completely happy
that Lina went
to college.
But she still spent
20 hours
at the car lot
every week.
That was important
to Al.

Also, Lina cooked meals
ahead of time.
The kids helped out
around the house.
Lina was keeping up
with everything
pretty well.
That was fine
with Al.

Sometimes things
did not go well
at school.
Sometimes Lina felt
much too busy.
Sometimes she
felt very tired.
Her life
went up and down.
But every time
she did well
on a test
or a paper,
Lina was sure
of one thing.
She was
on the right track.

Thinking It Over

1. Why is it still important
    to Lina
    that she please Al?

2. How do you know
    when you are
    "on the right track"?

3. What is it like
    to be different
    from the rest
    of the group?

4. Would you keep on
    doing something
    that was very hard for you?
    Why or why not?

CHAPTER 12

Winter break came.
Lina was glad
to have some time off
from school.
She could catch up
with some little jobs
around the house.

Before long,
it was time
to start classes again.

"Are you sure
you want to go back
to college?"
Al asked Lina.

"Of course,"
said Lina.
"I want to finish

what I started.
Besides, Al,
I like it!"

"Do you really
like it?"
Al asked.
"Sometimes I think
this whole thing
is killing you.
Wouldn't you rather
take it easy?"

"What for?"
said Lina.
"Then I would never have
what I want.
I want to finish school
and become a teacher.
I want that
more than anything
right now.
Now let me ask *you*
a question.

Did you ever
think about going
back to school?"

Al laughed.
"Me?" he said.
"Why should I
go to school?"

Lina told Al
about a night course
at the college.
It was called
"How to Make
More Money
from Your Business."
It was for people
who already had
a business.
They could learn
how to make their businesses
even better.
The class was
on Tuesday nights.

It would last
five weeks.

"It might be fun,"
Lina said.
"Why don't you
sign up?"

"I can't do that,"
said Al.
"I don't have
a high school diploma."

"You don't
need a diploma
for this course,"
said Lina.
"It's open
to anyone."

"Then maybe I will go,"
said Al.
"Maybe I just will.
You don't have to be

the only student
in this house
over the age of 18."

"Just one thing, Al,"
laughed Lina.
"Don't think
you'll get a new car
from me
if you pass
the business course!"

Now Al was smiling.
"Will you drive me
to school?"
he asked.
"Will you
open the door
for me?"

Lina smiled
at her husband.
"The door is open
for anyone,"

she said.
"Even an old-time person
like you!
All you have to do
is walk right in."

   "I think I know
what you mean,"
said Al.
"It just took me
a long time
to really understand."

   "And now you understand?"
asked Lina.

   "And now I do,"
said Al.

Thinking It Over

1. What does Lina mean
    when she says that Al
    is "an old-time person"?

2. Where can adults
    go to school
    in your town?
    What can they study?

3. What doors are open
    to you?